Nimrod & Semiramis

Nimrod

&

The Discovery In Erech

As I grew up in church and even well into adulthood, I heard man's sin after The Flood was their refusal to disperse and repopulate The Earth. It wasn't until recent years, my studies allowed me to discover something much more contrary to mainstream belief.

Genesis chapter ten is where we find what is known as The Table of Nations. In this text, we find a listing of seventy men descended from Noah and his three sons, Shem, Ham and Japheth. This is used for the basis of the belief there are only seventy God ordained Gentile nations. The 1611 King James tells us:

"...He fixed boundaries according to the sons of Israel."

Deut. 32:8, KJV1611

The Septuagint translation of The Old Testament tells us:

"When the Most High was apportioning nations, as He scattered Adam's sons, He fixed boundaries according to the number of divine sons."

Deut. 32:8, LXX

This verse tells us how God used angels and fixed the parameters of the nations of the world. Even *The Book of Jasher*, a 3,500 year old historical source, teaches us when The Tower of Babel fell, God sent seventy angels to aid in the destruction of The Tower:

"And God said to the seventy angels who stood foremost before him, to those who were near him, saying, Come, let us descend and confuse their tongues, that one man shall not understand the language of his neighbor, and they did so unto them."

Jasher 9:32

These seventy Gentile nations are believed to be matched by seventy Jewish providences within the twelve tribes of Israel which is based on the passage from Genesis chapter forty-six when Jacob moves his family to Egypt where Joseph is ruling. Jacob is listed with seventy of his descendants, including his grandson Job, who later lived in the land of Uz.

So, when did these seventy nations get formed? Was it really after the fall of The Tower of Babel? If so, how could everybody end up in precise places with confounded languages and at the same time so close to immediate family? Would they simply look for familiar faces of relatives and follow each other aimlessly or did everyone know where they were going before they were dispersed? Scripture, history and *The Book of Jubilees* tells us within the first century after The Flood, as men began to repopulate The Earth, settlements were made on the three major continental sections round The Mediterranean Sea[1]. Eventually, these major settlements became nations and carried the names of Noah's grandchildren[2]. Local settlements became the first cities and were named after Noah's great-grandchildren[3]. Let's look at what Scripture tells us:

---

[1] Gen. Ch. 10; Antiquities of the Jews 1.6.; Jubilees Ch. 8

[2] Gen. Ch. 10; Jubilees Ch. 9

[3] Jubilees 10:1-2

"These are the families of the sons of Noah, after their generations, in their nations and by these were the nations divided in the earth after the flood."

Gen. 10:32

What is often over looked in this passage is as subtle as it is obvious. This is the last verse just *before* the construction of The Tower of Babel in the first nine verses of Genesis chapter eleven. If you carefully look at history and other religious sources while balancing all information with Scripture, you will discover in the centuries which predated The Tower, the land was surveyed and divided among Noah's sons. Exactly 100 years after The Flood, a child was born from the lineage of Shem. His name was Peleg. The Bible tells us by the definition of Peleg's name, his birth and name commemorated the dividing of The Earth to Noah's three sons and their sons[4]. This would explain how everyone was so easily dispersed after the fall of The Tower of Babel — yet one question remains. If people had already dispersed, what brought everyone back to The Land of Shinar?

Before we answer this question, we must first profile the life of a very important individual who was coming of age during this time. His name is Nimrod.

Genesis tells us:

"... Cush begat Nimrod: he began to be a mighty one in the earth. He was a mighty hunter before the Lord..."

Gen. 10:8-9

---

[4] Gen. 10:25

As we can see from Scripture, Nimrod *began* to be a mighty one in The Earth...but what does *that* mean? It would appear from Scripture Nimrod was one type of being then became something else. Was it just a mighty hunter as we think? Did he just have a good track record with wildlife or was something else in play here?

According to history, Nimrod is not the man we have all come to love to hate in The Church. *The Book of Jasher* tells us:

"And in their going out [from The Ark] Ham stole those garments [that were handed down from Adam which he had received from God] from Noah his father... and when Ham had begat his firstborn Cush, He gave him the garments in secret... and when Cush had begotten Nimrod, he gave him those garments... and when Nimrod ... was twenty years old he put on those garments. And Nimrod became strong when he put on the garments, and he was a mighty hunter in the earth, yea, he was a mighty hunter in the field, and he hunted the animals and he built altars, and he offered upon them the animals before the Lord."

Jasher 7:27, 29
brackets added by author

Here in *The Book of Jasher,* we see almost the same wording as in Genesis and the credit of Nimrod's power is given to these garments made by God! You might ask can something touched by God give supernatural abilities? Apparently so. Luke tells us in Acts:

"... God wrought special miracles by the hands of Paul. So that from his body were brought unto the sick handkerchiefs or aprons, and the diseases departed from them, and the evil spirits went out of them."

Acts 19:11-12

In this portion of Scripture, we are told articles of Paul's clothing were used to heal the sick and cast out demons after The Holy Spirit came in contact with Paul!

Now that we know how Nimrod became mighty and that he once served The Lord, but how did he become catapulted into global status? *The Book of Jasher* gives the answer:

"And when Nimrod was forty years old, at that time there was a war between his brethren [= the children of Ham] and the children of Japheth... and Nimrod went forth at that time, and he assembled all the sons of Cush and their families... and he went with them into battle and... Nimrod strengthened the hearts of the people that went with him....and they [= The Hamites] fought against their enemies and they destroyed them and subdued them and Nimrod placed standing officers over them in their respective places. And when Nimrod had joyfully returned from battle, after having conquered his enemies, all his brethern... assembled to make him king over them, and they placed a regal crown upon his head."

Jasher 7:34-35, 37, 39
brackets added by author

We learn several things from this piece of history. First, the nations were already established. Secondly, a great war — the first World War in Earth's history — broke out. Third, Nimrod led his brethren not just into battle but also into victory. Fourth, this one event catapulted Nimrod into a world leader status. Later in this same chapter, we learn Nimrod moved his seat of authority from The Land of Cush to The Land of Shinar[5] and eventually under the advice of his mighty men, he oversaw the construction of The Tower of Babel[6] and he was the first to make gods of wood and stone and worship them[7]. The Tower of Babel was an attempt to maintain order after a global war. This is paralleled with the formation of The League of Nations just after World War I, which would eventually lead to the creation of The United Nations. Ironically, Nimrod's World War was in the early to mid-twentieth century after the first Adam just as our World Wars were in the early to mid-twentieth century after The Second Adam, Jesus Christ!

Now the next question to be answered is *"Why Shinar?"*. What made our ancestors choose The Land of Shinar to place their ancient capitol? Was it just an act of defiance against God or was it because The Land of Shinar was centrally located to the rest of the known world? I believe the truth to be far darker and much more sinister than what is traditionally taught.

Genesis tells us Peleg was born 100 years after The Flood. It was at this time cities were being built. *The Book of Jubilees* also tells us evil spirits influenced mankind as cities were built:

---

[5] Jasher 7:44

[6] Jasher 7:42-43

[7] Jasher 7:47

"The sons of Noah... told him about the demons that were leading astray and blinding and slaying his sons' sons."

Jubilees 10:2

"The sons of Noah began to war with each other, ... and to build strong cities, and walls, and towers, ... "

Jubilees 11:2

<u>The Book of Jubilees</u> also tells us about the exploits of one of the most infamous men in the immediate post-flood period. His name is Canaan. According to Genesis, Canaan was curse by Noah[8] and in the Gospel of Luke, we discover Canaan is in the lineage of Jesus Christ[9]. <u>The Book of Jubilees</u> tells us:

"The son [= Canaan] grew, and his father taught him writing, and he went to seek for himself a place where he might seize a city for himself. He found writing which former generations had carved on a rock, and he read what was on it, and he transcribed it and sinned because of it, for it contained the teaching of The Watchers, which they had used to observe the omens of the sun and moon and stars in all the signs of heaven."

Jubilees 8:2-4
brackets added by author

Is there any evidence in Scripture to this alleged archaeological search? Surprisingly, yes. Let's begin our word study. Let me make one thing perfectly clear — I am *not* adding to The Word of God. I *am* using the original Hebrew language

---

[8] Gen. 9:25

[9] Lk. 3:36

to better define and amplify the text for our understanding. Here is what we get from a Hebrew word study from Genesis chapter eleven:

1. Language (v. 1) = speech
2. Speech (v. 1) = parts of speech
3. Journeyed (v. 2) = [to] leave; to be pulled up or out; to lead
4. Found (v. 2) = to find, find out, to discover; cause to encounter; to find favor in the eyes [of someone]
5. Tower (v. 4, 5) = tower; watchtower; a tall narrow building for defense; an elevated garden with mounds and terraces
6. Top (v. 4) = head; high status or authority; leader
7. Heaven (v. 4) = the abode of the stars; the invisible realm of God
8. Will be restrained (v. 6) = to be impossible; thwarted
9. Have imagined (v. 6) = to determine; plan; plot; resovled
10. Confound (v. 7) = to confuse; to mix
11. Understand (v. 7) = to summon; call together

Now let's read the Genesis account of The Tower of Babel with these added definitions and see what the text is actually saying:

"And the whole earth was of one language [speech] and of one speech [parts of speech]. And it came to pass, as the journeyed [were lead (this would imply they came from the west)] from the east that they found [favour in the eyes (of demons?) and were caused to encounter or discover] a plain in the land of Shinar and they dwelt there.

And they said one to another Go to, let us make brick, and burn them thoroughly. And they had brick for stone, and slime they had for mortar. And they said Go to, let us build a city and a tower [watchtower for defense (designed as an) elevated garden with terraces] whose top [leader(s)] may reach unto heaven [outer space; the realm of God; (other demensions?)] and let us make a name, lest we be scattered abroad from the face of the whole earth.

And the Lord came down to see the city and tower [watchtower for defense (designed as an) elevated garden with terraces], which the children of men builded. And the Lord said, Behold, the people is one, and they all have one language; and this they begin to do: now nothing will be restrained [impossible; thwarted] from them, which they have imagined [resolved] to do. Go to, let us go down, and there confound [confuse; mix] their language, that they may not understand [summond; call together] one another's speech. So the Lord scattered them abroad from thence upon the face of all the earth: and they left off to build the city. Therefore is the name of it called Babel; because the Lord did confound the language of all the earth: and from thence did the Lord scatter them abroad upon the face of the earth."

Gen. 11:1-9
brackets added by author

This is most profound when we consider the original meanings of these key words. Though Nimrod was an idolater, The Tower of Babel appeared to have the primary purpose of war as modeled after a garden. To me, this is strong evidence of Lucifer's direct influence on the early post-flood patriarchs. Remember, Lucifer used to dwell on the holy mountain of God in The Garden of God[10]. This would explain the garden-like nature of this particular watchtower prepared for a defensive strike. Furthermore, Lucifer promised he would ascend into heaven, exalt his throne above God's and sit upon the mountain of the congregation[11]. The Hebrew word for *"congregation"* is defined as *"appointed time"*. Lucifer is planning a precise attack on the throne of God!

In the story of The Tower of Babel, we have evidence its construction actually started as an archaeological search. This is exactly what is described as Canaan's actions in *The Book of Jubilees* and is preserved in the original Hebrew text. The actual discovery of forbidden knowledge of The Watchers from the pre-flood world is also supported by the original Hebrew.

The Book of Jubilees tells us the sons of Noah told him of his children's plight. Noah very well could have begun to intercede through prayer on behalf of his offspring who had become slaves to Nimrod. This fervent prayer would have summoned The Lord to come down and set the captives free! This is not a story told in church but supported by Scripture, history and religious writings and may very well be the most accurate rendering of what really happened 4,000 years ago in ancient Iraq.

---

[10] Ezek. 28:13-14

[11] Isa. 14:13

While all this was going on, a young man, who was destined to change the course of history, was living with Noah. His name was Abram. The world would know him as Abraham.

One famous myth from antiquity is _The Epic of Gilgamesh_. The hero of this _myth_ has more than just a few startling similarities to the biblical villain Nimrod. Anyone who has ever studied the text clearly points out Gilgamesh and Nimrod are one and the same.

One of the many events documented in this tale is the long journey taken by Gilgamesh/Nimrod to see Utnapishtim, a wise old man who survived a worldwide deluge after being warning of the coming catastrophe by the gods and commanded to build a large boat and load it with animals a various kinds. Obviously, Utnapishtim is the biblical Noah. One detail about this particular character told in this epic is the pre-flood home of Utnapishtim/Noah known as Shurrupak which was located on the river Euphrates. This same river was one of the boundaries of The Garden of Eden[12]. According to one Jewish tradition from _The Book of the Cave of Treasures_, Noah lived in the geographical location of The Garden of Eden.

Gilgamesh is The Sumerian equivalent of the biblical Nimrod. Both were warriors who conquered beast[13], man[14], woman[15]

---

[12] Gen. 2:10-14

[13] _The Book of Jasher_ teaches Nimrod up until the age of twenty was a skilled hunter who built altars and made sacrifices unto The Lord (Jasher 7:29-30). The book of Genesis also confirms Nimrod's ability to hunt (Gen. 10:9).

[14] _The Book of Jasher_ teaches Nimrod led the children of Ham into war against the children of Japheth (Jasher 7:31-39).

[15] _The Epic of Gilgamesh_ tells us Gilgamesh's _"...lust leaves no virgin to her lover, neither the warrior's daughter nor the wife of the noble..."_(_The Epic of Gilgamesh_, chapter one: The Coming of Enkidu, page 62, Penguin Classics, ISBN-13: 978-0-140-44100-0).

and child[16]. Both were kings. Both were involved in building cities and a tower for centralized worship. Gilgamesh, however, had a companion fashioned from the gods. Gilgamesh even had the goddess Ishtar fall in love with him. Nimrod is said to have married a woman named Semiramis who was later deified as a goddess often times associated with The Greek goddess Aphrodite.

Gilgamesh, according to the myth, was $2/3$ god and $1/3$ mortal. Both The Bible and *The Book of Jasher* names Cush, son of Ham, son of Noah as Nimrod's father. Since Cush was human, this would mean, if the myth can be trusted, Nimrod's mother was a goddess. Gilgamesh's family tree would have looked like this:

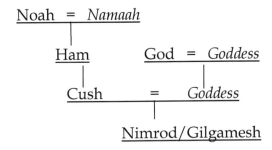

So, who was this goddess who was Nimrod's mother? Could Nimrod's mother have been an angel? Could she have been one of The Watchers who descended to The Earth? If so, when did she descend? Didn't the Watchers descend before The Flood get condemned to Tartarus prior to The Flood? Did she escape from Hell? Was there a second descent of angels? Was there a second fall of angels? Perhaps she was just a mortal woman who had extra longevity and really good genetics giving her extended youth and super strength which, when combined, caused others to see her as a goddess as the case was so often back then. What does myth and legend tells us? More importantly, what does The Bible teach us? History changes every day but doctrine never changes. The Word of God is solid…even more so than the foundations of the world! Whatever theory one formulates must be biblically sound and even in the smallest way, it must parallel with myth and legend.

First let's address the gender of angels. Are there female angels?

We may never know.

Ham lived to be about 600 years old. Cush's generation would have lived to the age of 400. Nimrod only lived to the age of 215 before he was assassinated by Esau. Since Nimrod and those younger than him would not have lived as long as those in previous generations, the older generations could easily have been looked upon as gods and goddesses. However, Cush should have also been considered a god. This would make Nimrod, who was Gilgamesh, 100% god unless his mother was much younger than Cush. This leads us to an alternative view of Gilgamesh's status of deity. The Bible tells us:

"And Cush begot Nimrod: he began to be a mighty one in the earth. He was a mighty hunter before The Lord: wherefore it is said, 'Even as Nimrod the mighty hunter before The Lord."

Gen. 10:8-9

The Hebrew word for *"began"* is defined as *"top defile one's self; to pierce, to wound; to play the flute"*. This would imply Nimrod "defiled himself by being pierced [as if by a demon]". The Hebrew term used in this verse for *"mighty hunter"* is *"gibbor"* as is closely associated with the terms used in The New Testament when referring to demons! It is also translated in Genesis six as *"mighty men"* in referenced to The Nephilim:

"There were giants in the Earth in those days and also after that, when the sons of God came into the daughters of men, the same became <u>mighty men</u> which were of old, men of reknown."

Gen. 6:4
underline added by author

Nimrod may have been genetically altered by forbidden knowledge discovered by Canaan, Nimrod's uncle. This makes a very interesting genealogical sketch and profile for Nimrod—albeit, a theoretical one. Nimrod is a type of The Anti-Christ and since the coming Anti-Christ will come from this ancient Babylonian empire, the question begs to be asked. *Will The Anti-Christ be a nephilim or perhaps claim an extra-terrestrial origin of some sort?*

In Scripture, when Noah became drunk, Ham uncovered Noah's nakedness. The Hebrew text tells us by this act of exposing his father's nakedness, Ham actually revealed Noah's nakedness.

According to _The Book of Jasher_, Ham stole his garments. These were the very garments God had made for Adam and Eve back in The Garden of Eden. Noah received these garments from Methuselah, who received them from Enoch who received them from Adam! After Ham had taken these special garments from Noah, he hid them many years until the son of his old age was grown. When he turned twenty years of age, Nimrod put on these garments made by the hand of God. Could wearing garments made directly by the hand of God have altered Nimrod in some way that magnified his basic human traits? If so, this would account for him becoming a mighty man—someone with supernatural endurance of god-like proportions!

Gilgamesh, unlike what we know about Nimrod from Scripture and history, actually went on a quest to discover the secrets of eternal life. This part of this particular myth lends credibility to a belief Nimrod had an interest in immortality. Since he was twenty when he first wore Adam's special garments, this event in Gilgamesh's life may have occurred when he—that is Nimrod—was just a teenager! Where did he set his journey for? The home of his father Utnapishtim who survived a global deluge by building a large boat. Nimrod's father was Cush who was born _after_ The Flood. Obviously, Cush is not Utnapishtim but Nimrod's grandfather and great-grandfather did build a boat and survived The Flood. Respectively, these two men are Ham and Noah. Either are prime candidates for the historical Utnapishtim mentioned in the famous epic. According to _The Book of Jasher_, and Scripture, Noah—as was his son Ham—was a contemporary with both Nimrod and Abraham.

What would give Gilgamesh the desire to seek out the secrets of eternal life? According to *The Epic of Gilgamesh*, the hero had a friend named Enkidu. Enkidu was created by the gods and lived in the mountains among wildlife and was covered with hair from head to toe. Enkidu is the earliest recording of what we today would call a Bigfoot or Sasquatch. After a great battle against The Bull from Heaven, in response to Gilgamesh rejecting the goddess Ishtar's advances, Enkidu becomes sick and dies. Grieved, Gilgamesh sets out on his famous quest. Even today, when we are faced with death, we will question our own mortality…but is this just simply a mourning process for Gilgamesh?

According to the legend, Gilgamesh, also known as Nimrod, went on a long and grueling journey. The text seems to imply he was not just seeking *not* to die. When he finally arrives at Utnapishtim's home, he is questioned on his condition. Gilgamesh appears to be much older and worn out more than others during his own time. Look at what history and Scripture says about the longevity of mankind during the different centuries following The Flood:

Patriarch	Age at Death	Reference
1. Noah	950	Gen. 9:29
2. Shem	600	Gen. 11:10-11
3. Araphaxad	438	Gen. 11:12-13
4. Peleg	239	Gen. 11:18-19
5. Nimrod	215	Jasher 27:7-9
6. Abraham	175	Gen. 25:7-8

Based on Scripture alone, you can see in the first three hundred years after The Flood, human longevity quickly diminished. When Noah died in the year 2006 after creation[17] at the age of 950, Abraham was only fifty-five years old. Nimrod was just ninety-five years old. If Nimrod is the mythical Gilgamesh, this epic journey would have taken place around the year 1928 after creation[18] when Nimrod would have been about twenty years old. Noah would have been 830 years old. Peleg would have been 173 years old. Can you just imagine how you might view human existence if you were only twenty years old and you looked fifty? Peleg, at age 173, would have looked as good as Nimrod, at age 30 — and Noah and his wife would have looked even better at over 800 years old! I believe with human life expectancy dropping rapidly, genetics deteriating, the death of his best friend and those who were ancient looking like they were in the prime of their life challenged Gilgamesh/Nimrod to seek the "secrets" to eternal life. When Gilgamesh/Nimrod left Utnapishtim/Noah's home, there is no evidence he left rejoicing over a renewed life in The One True Living God. *The Epic of Gilgamesh* implies just the opposite and Scripture also tells the opposite[19]. I believe the evidence is strong for Nimrod and Noah being Gilgamesh and Utnapishtim, respectively.

Gilgamesh was the historical Nimrod, builder of The Tower of Babel, infamous military genius and inventor of slavery. He was the adversary of Abraham and a contemporary with Noah. His tomb was discovered in Iraq in 2003.

---

[17] 1994 B.C.

[18] Approximately 2072 B.C.

[19] Cf. Gen. 10:8-9; The word *"began"* in this verse implies a physiological change in Nimrod causing him to deviate from a path of righteousness.

Semiramis

What of the legends and traditions? These are trickier to deal with than just having to simply sift through historical facts and propaganda because they almost never have any roots that can be traced to a real event therefore, they remain obscure shadows of historical mystery. This is the case of Semiramis, wife of Nimrod, builder of The Tower of Babel. According to tradition and legend, Nimrod ruled for half a century (fifty-two years by some accounts) before he died and his wife, Semiramis, ruled after him for forty-two years before she died totaling a period of 102 years for her time of reign. Semiramis is believed to have also been of royal descent, yet she worked in a brothel in the city of Erech. It is also believed she initiated much of what we now know as various false religions in the world today but what does history and The Bible say?

First of all, Semiramis is mentioned *nowhere* in Scripture. Furthermore, Nimrod is not even mentioned as having a wife at The Tower of Babel. According to *The Book of Jasher*, we know Nimrod was forty years old when he came to power at the time of the building of The Tower of Babel just after a great war involving Europe and Africa. It took forty-eight years of building before The Lord came down and confounded the languages putting an end to its construction. During this time, Terah, Abraham's father, was the religious leader at The Tower of Babel. Nimrod lived another 127 years before he was decapitated by Esau, Abraham's grandson. These are biblical and historical facts. Where does Semiramis fit into these facts?

Historians and theologians who claim she was married to Nimrod place her at The Tower of Babel and her mystery religion started after the death of Nimrod. If she was a real historical figure and married to Nimrod, it wasn't *necessarily* at the time of The Tower because Nimrod lived over a century past the dispersion at The Tower. Legend states Semiramis lived forty-two years after the death of Nimrod completing her 102 years total reign. If Nimrod died 127 years after The Dispersion[20], this changes the date of Semiramis' solo reign and further gives us an exact date of when she did marry Nimrod, commencing a century long rule.

Upon returning from Europe, Nimrod brought back slaves—many were children[21]. Semiramis may have been a child slave fully stripped of her royal birthright. Eventually, she could have gained her *"freedom"* and

---

[20] The Tower of Babel was destroyed in the year 1996 After Creation (2004 B.C.) and Nimrod was killed in the year 2123 after creation (1977 B.C.).

[21] Jasher 7:38

became a prostitute in one of Nimrod's chief cities—Erech[22]. This would lead to their meeting and eventual marriage—or rather consorting—years after the fall of The Tower of Babel. This being easily proven would have ended her rule in the year 2165 after creation. Since this would be 102 years after she married Nimrod, this places their marriage in the year 2063 after creation. This would have been sixty-nine years after the fall of The Tower of Babel. Therefore, we can easily conclude Semiramis had nothing to do with The Tower whatsoever. Her illegitimate son, Tammuz, would have been born in the year 2124 after creation and he would have been a contemporary with Jacob and Esau though he would have been fifteen years younger and in the years to come, he would grow up and possibly even rose to power in The Land of Shinar where Nimrod and his mother, Semiramis, had ruled.

Semiramis would have struggled to maintain her authority because *The Book of Jasher* teaches Nimrod's kingdom was divided at his death[23]—something the legend of Semiramis refers to. In an attempt to maintain political power during a turbulent time of Sumerian politics, Semiramis would have developed the concept of re-incarnation of Nimrod into her yet unborn son through a false religion based on further manipulation of the zodiac and ancestor worship[24] which was originated by Canaan, Nimrod's uncle and father of the Canaanites, prior to the building of The Tower of Babel and taught by Terah, Abraham's father.

Semiramis became associated with many goddesses in many pantheons around the world. She has been referred to as Isis of Egypt, Aphrodite of Greece, Venus of Rome and Ishtar of the Babylonians just to name a few. For simplification, I will focus on the Greco-Roman culture in this essay.

Who was Aphrodite? If your knowledge of this ancient goddess is limited to a junior high or high school level of education, everything you know about her just might be wrong. Aphrodite is her Greek name whereas in The Roman culture, she was known as Venus and associated with the

---

[22] Gen. 10:8-10

[23] Jasher 27:16-17

[24] Gen. 4:25-26; Jasher 2:2-5

second planet of our solar system. She is given the title of *"goddess of love"* but nothing could be further than the truth.

Some very interesting characteristics of this deity include a perpetual youthful appearance, blue eyes and blonde hair. She was known as *"The Mother of Laughter"* and associated with sexual inhibition and unbridled passion. Flowers grew in her footsteps. Her main lover—which she had many—was Ares. Mars was his Roman name. Ares was an extremely violent deity who loved carnage and war. Aphrodite was a sexually perverse goddess. These two would have undoubtedly had a sadomasochistic relationship. Aphrodite was famous for not just her sexual exploits but also for provoking individuals into fatal combat for a chance to be with her. She would then reserve the option to reject the winner despite the bloodshed. Aphrodite was unique in the sense she had power not just power over male *and* female but man and god alike.

Aphrodite had two children that stand out. Through Ares, she conceived Eros. His Roman name was Cupid. Eros is The Greek word for *"carnal love"*—far from the agape love Christ has shown toward us. Eros, that is Cupid, had a lover, Psyche. Psyche is The Greek word for the human spirit. Eros was not exactly kind to her...but then again, what else would you expect based on his lineage? Aphrodite conceived another son with Hermes (Mercury in Roman myth). Their son eventually merged with another individual and maintained both sexes even today. His name was a combination of both his father and mother's name—Hermaphrodite. This title has been given to those having both male and female sets of sexual organs. Hermes had several other offspring including Pan, a male satyr who was fond of young mortal women as well as animals.

The followers of Aphrodite were also associated with Dionysus. During *The Festival of Dionysia*, females would dance naked in drunken bliss and engaged in acts sexual freedom and ate raw meat while using various forms of substances whether it be alcohol or drugs as they expressed themselves in the most carnal ways imaginable. Aphrodite's temples where also associated with prostitution.

When Nimrod conquered Europe during the first post flood global war, he brought back slaves—many of them just children. Aphrodite, according to some myths, was the daughter of Zeus, who, according to some legends, was Japheth, son of Noah, father of all Europeans. Some say she was born from the castrated sexual member of Uranus, the supreme god of all gods, when his son Cronus attacked him. Either way, Aphrodite would have had a "royal" lineage and she would have had a godly upbringing. This is exactly what legend says about Semiramis. I'll let you read Psalm chapter two for some surprising parallels to be found there. Furthermore, blonde hair and blue eyes are European characteristics. Aphrodite is said to have led a very promiscuous life style, much like the adult Semiramis who became a harlot.

So, what do we do with this ancient pervert? Why should she be considered relevant in our modern world? Consider this: In 1917 Fatima, Portugal, The Apparitions of (the Virgin) Mary began. Some little known facts about Mary as she is portrayed in these apparitions are:

1. She is perpetual youthful in appearance.
2. She has blonde hair and blue eyes.
3. Flowers often grow where the apparition stands and if the vision occurs in the sky, flowers rain down on viewers.
4. She seeks to be worshiped.

Every one of these characteristics is descriptive of Aphrodite! Look at how John describes The Tribulation *"church"*:

"...the kings of the earth have committed fornication, and the inhabitants of the earth have been made drunk with the wine of her fornication. And upon her forehead was a name written, MYSTERY BABYLON THE GREAT, THE MOTHER OF HARLOTS AND ABOMINATIONS OF THE EARTH. And I saw the woman drunken with the blood of the saint and the martyrs of Jesus: and when I saw her, I wondered with great admiration."
Rev. 17:2, 5-6

Notice, the characteristics of this bride[25] turned whore: fornication, harlotry, drunkenness and bloodshed. All terms used to describe both

---

[25] The Greek word for *"woman"* throughout the book of Revelation is *"gyne"* and is defined as *"a woman (129x in The New Testament); a wife (92x in The New Testament)"*. I believe the woman in Revelation chapter twelve is the nation of Israel because Israel brought forth The Messiah however, the religious system of Revelation seventeen is nconsidered to be not just a woman but a bride. The Church is the *ONLY* religious system in the world known as being a bride.

Aphrodite and Semiramis and in the prophetic role of the Mary of Roman Catholicism! I believe there is ample evidence to support the legacy of Semiramis *is* found in the personification of Aphrodite and the spirit behind her has returned in the form of Roman Catholicism.

The Return of Semiramis

First of all, let me say I do not believe in re-incarnation. Semiramis will not return now that she has died. I do believe, however, a spirit that has laid claim to her memory and will—and has—returned from the ancient land of Shinar.

There was a time when The Church was united but about 500 years ago, a rift between many who were seeking discipleship through the guiding of The Holy Spirit and a serious study of The Word of God began to clash with political leaders within the church body. This rift gave rise to what we today now refer to as the two factions of Christianity—Protestants and Catholics.

Many Protestants believe this rift could never happen again...but Paul warns us against such boasting. Paul tells us of a coming time when the church will have:

"...a form of godliness but denying the power thereof..."

2Tim . 3:5

Paul also tell us:

"...the time will come when they will not endure sound doctrine; but after their own lusts shall they heap to themselves teachers, having itching ears; and they shall turn away their ears from the truth, and shall be turned unto fables."

2Tim. 4:3-4

Jesus warns us against those who:

"...come unto you in sheep's clothing, but inwardly they are ravening wolves."

Matt. 7:15

Sheep only exist within the folds of The Church. Today, more and more churches follow man rather than God. They seek personas over fellowship. When it gets to the point when churches are dependent on individuals for either doctrines or financial support or both, it's a sign

Christ is no longer the center of worship nor the sole provider for the local body. Paul prophesied when he said:

"...after my departing shall grievous wolves enter in among you, not sparing the flock."

Acts 20:29

The book of Revelation mentions a woman who rides The Beast, a whore. According to The Greek language, this *"woman"* is a *"bride"*. The only religious system in the world who calls herself a bride is The Church. This is clear evidence the end-time church is playing the role of whore against her Bridegroom, Jesus Christ!

Dark times are coming on America as a dawning of spiritual awakening and revival is breaking forth! Church, be sober and watchful. I leave with these words:

"Be ye therefore ready also: for the Son of man cometh at an hour when ye think not."

Lk. 12:40

"...when these things begin to come to pass, look up, and lift your heads for your redemption draweth nigh."

Lk. 21:28

Closing Thoughts

Many people have concluded that Nimrod is every other god, demi-god and hero of ancient mythology just as Semiramis is believed to be the corresponding goddess to each god. On the following pages, you will find a family tree proving Nimrod is not every god who was worshiped in ages past. My sources are The Bible, _The Book of Jasher_ and _The Antiquities of the Jews_, each respected and reliable historical sources. A timeline is also included showing both dates before Christ (BC) and after creation (AC).

Is Nimrod:

—Osiris? No. Osiris was Noah's great-great-grandson, father to Hagar and grandfather to Ishmael. Osiris was Egyptian whereas Nimrod was Ethiopian.

—Hercules? No. Hercules lived centuries after The Tower of Babel. He led a military campaign against Africa just prior to The Exodus and married Abraham's great-great-granddaughter.

—Ares/Mars? Yes. Both Ares and Nimrod were associated with war and conquest. Ares was the least loved of the Greco-Roman gods which is something that would be expected since Nimrod was not European and conquered all of early post-flood Europe. Ares was associated with Aphrodite/Venus, a goddess of promiscuity and prostitution who was fond of revelry while using drugs and alcohol. Semiramis was a prostitute fond of revelry.

—Gilgamesh? Yes. Gilgamesh was also associated with war and conquest but not just of nations but also animals, man, woman and child. He was also associated with Ishtar, a Sumerian goddess of seduction.

Genealogy of Gods, Demigods and Mortals of Myth and History

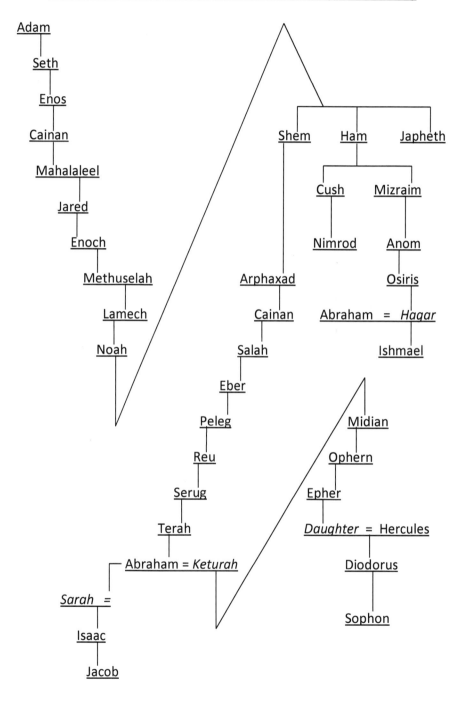

Scripture and Historical References

1. Adam to Noah (Gen. Ch. 5)
2. Noah's sons (Gen. 11:1)
3. Shem to Abraham (Gen. 11:11-26)
   a) Cainan (Lk. 3:36)
   b) Abraham and Sarah's descendants (Gen. 11:29; 21:2-3; 25:25-26)
   c) Abraham and Keturah's descendants (Gen. 25:1, 4)
   d) Hercules (Antiquities of the Jews 1.15)
4. Ham's sons (Gen. 10:1, 6)
   a) Nimrod (Gen. 10:6-8)
   b) Osiris (Jasher 14:1-2; 15:31-32)

Chronology of Nimrod & Semiramis

AC	BC	Event
1656	2344	The Flood.
1756	2244	Peleg born.
1908	2092	Nimrod born.
1928	2072	Nimrod becomes a mighty man.
1948	2052	Nimrod leads his brethren into battle against early post-flood European settlements; Abraham born.
1958	2042	Construction on The Tower of Babel begins.
1995	2005	The Tower of Babel is destroyed; Peleg, age 239, dies.
2006	2004	Noah, age 950, dies.
2023	1977	The call of Abraham.
2048	1952	Isaac born.
2063	1937	Nimrod and Semiramis marry.
2084	1916	Abraham and Isaac go to Mount Moriah.
2088	1912	Isaac and Rebekah marry.
2108	1892	Jacob and Esau born.
2123	1877	Abraham, age 175, dies; Nimrod, age 215, is assassinated by Esau, age 15.
2158	1842	Shem, age 600, dies.
2165	1835	Semiramis dies.

ABOUT THE AUTHOR

Micheal was born and raised in north Alabama. He grew up and went to school in Oxford, Alabama and in February of 1986, he received Jesus Christ as his Savior while attending a week long revival at the Salvation Army church in the neighboring city of Anniston.

After graduating Oxford High School in 1988, Micheal joined the navy for four years and served as a torpedo man's mate onboard two nuclear submarines – the U.S.S. Jack (SSN 605) and the U.S.S. Billfish (SSN 676). During Desert Storm, he developed a renewed interest in biblical studies as ancient Babylon began to come to the forefront of current events again.

In the early 1990s, Micheal moved to St. Petersburg, Florida and in the spring of 1999, he attended his first *God's News Behind the News International Prophecy Conference* which only fueled his interest in biblical studies. Micheal still lives in St. Petersburg and is a member of Gateway Christian Center.

Other books by Micheal:

As It Was In the Days of Noah and the Days of Lot
The Days of Sodom & Gomorrah
The Biblical Origin of Pagan Mythology
Activity Book

To order more copies of this book go to
www.CreateSpace.com
To contact Micheal: **mcleorising69@aol.com**

For a quality television drama for the whole family, check out *Walk On Water*. See your local listings on Christian television or check us out on the web at www.WalkOnWater.tv and follow us on FaceBook at "Walk On Water: The Television Series".

Made in the USA
Middletown, DE
21 January 2024

48293838R00029